ROSA
PARKS

By Joan Stoltman

Gareth Stevens
PUBLISHING

Please visit our website, www.garethstevens.com. For a free color catalog of all our high-quality books, call toll free 1-800-542-2595 or fax 1-877-542-2596.

Library of Congress Cataloging-in-Publication Data
Names: Stoltman, Joan, author.
Title: Rosa Parks / Joan Stoltman.
Description: New York : Gareth Stevens Publishing, 2018. | Series: Little
  biographies of big people | Includes index.
Identifiers: LCCN 2017023602| ISBN 9781538209332 (pbk.) | ISBN 9781538209349 (6 pack) |
ISBN 9781538209356 (library bound)
Subjects: LCSH: Parks, Rosa, 1913-2005–Juvenile literature. | African
  American women–Alabama–Montgomery–Biography–Juvenile literature. |
  African Americans–Alabama–Montgomery–Biography–Juvenile literature. |
  Civil rights workers–Alabama–Montgomery–Biography–Juvenile literature.
  | African Americans–Civil rights–Alabama–Montgomery–History–20th
  century–Juvenile literature. | Segregation in
  transportation–Alabama–Montgomery–History–20th century–Juvenile
  literature. | Montgomery (Ala.)–Race relations–Juvenile literature. |
  Montgomery (Ala.)–Biography–Juvenile literature.
Classification: LCC F334.M753 S76 2018 | DDC 323.092 [B] –dc23
LC record available at https://lccn.loc.gov/2017023602

Published in 2018 by
Gareth Stevens Publishing
111 East 14th Street, Suite 349
New York, NY 10003

Designer: Samantha DeMartin
Editor: Joan Stoltman

Photo credits: series art Yulia Glam/Shutterstock.com; Cover, p. 1 William Philpott/Hulton Archive/Getty Images; p. 5 MassiveEartha/Wikimedia Commons; pp. 7, 11, 17 Bettmann/Bettmann/Getty Images; p. 9 (main) Library of Congress/Corbis Historical/Getty Images; p. 9 (inset) The Washington Post/The Washington Post/Getty Images; p. 13 UniversalImagesGroup/Universal Images Group/Getty Images; p. 15 Grey Villet/The LIFE Picture Collection/Getty Images; p. 19 Taro Yamasaki/The LIFE Images Collection/Getty Images; p. 21 BRENDAN SMIALOWSKI/AFP/Getty Images.

Printed in the United States of America

CPSIA compliance information: Batch #CW18GS: For further information contact Gareth Stevens, New York, New York at 1-800-542-2595.

CONTENTS

Boldface words appear in the glossary.

Born in Troubled Times

Rosa Parks was born in 1913 in Alabama. When she was young, she moved into her grandparents' house with her mother and brother, Sylvester. Her grandparents were both former slaves. Rosa was born years after slavery ended, but black people were still treated badly.

Rosa grew up during **segregation**. Black people had separate elevators, restrooms, entrances, and even drinking fountains. A black person could get hurt or killed for not following the laws and **customs** of the South. Rosa's black school had only one room and one teacher for 50 students of all ages.

An Early Leader

At age 19, Rosa married Raymond Parks. He was a member of the National Association for the Advancement of Colored People (NAACP). Rosa joined, too! With the NAACP, Rosa helped work for black voting rights, fair treatment from police and judges, and to end segregation.

JOIN N.A.A.C.P. NOW

Raymond Parks

The Day Everything Changed

One day in 1955, Rosa was riding the bus home from work. In the South, black people had to sit in the back of the bus. Whites could sit in the front. But once the front was full, the bus driver tried to give Rosa's seat to a white person. She wouldn't allow it.

"I was not tired **physically**... No, the only tired I was, was tired of giving in."

- Rosa Parks

The bus driver called the police. Rosa was taken off the bus and put in jail. It wasn't the first time a black person had stood up against segregation. But her friends at the NAACP decided it would be the last.

7053

13

"A Change Is Gonna Come"

The local NAACP group met to organize a bus **boycott**. They placed ads in newspapers and passed out flyers in black neighborhoods, churches, and schools. It wasn't easy, but 40,000 black people **carpooled**, biked, walked, and even rode mules instead of riding the bus.

15

The bus boycott in Montgomery, Alabama, was the first time so many people stood up against segregation. Rosa, Dr. Martin Luther King Jr., and 87 others were jailed for boycotting. Yet the boycott continued for over a year until the city changed its laws!

Dr. Martin Luther King Jr.

Continuing to Fight

After segregation was made illegal, Rosa and Raymond moved to Detroit, Michigan. Rosa continued to fight for equal treatment of blacks and women in schools, housing, jobs, and the courts. She also taught many young people about history and how to be good citizens.

Rosa died at age 92 in 2005. She's the only woman to ever **lie in state** at the Capitol in Washington, DC. In 2013, a statue of her was built at the Capitol. Rosa was one person who made a big difference!

"Freedom fighters never retire."
- Rosa Parks

21

GLOSSARY

boycott: the act of refusing to have dealings with a person or business in order to force change

carpool: to share a car with other people to travel for jobs or school

custom: a way of doing things that is usual among the people in a certain group or place

lie in state: when the body of a famous leader is displayed in a public place so that people can view it and show respect

physically: having to do with the body

segregation: the forced separation of races or classes

FOR MORE INFORMATION

BOOKS

Hansen, Grace. *Rosa Parks: Activist for Equality*. Minneapolis, MN: ABDO Kids, 2016.

Jazynka, Kitson. *Rosa Parks*. Washington, DC: National Geographic, 2015.

Meltzer, Brad. *I Am Rosa Parks*. New York, NY: Dial Books for Young Readers, 2014.

WEBSITES

Rosa Parks Gallery
achievement.org/achiever/rosa-parks/#gallery
See many important photographs from throughout Rosa Parks's life.

Rosa Parks Sparks Bus Boycott
biography.com/video/rosa-parks-sparks-bus-boycott-34625563
Watch this video about what happened after Rosa Parks took a stand.

Standing Up for Freedom
achievement.org/achiever/rosa-parks/#interview
Watch this video interview of Rosa Parks in 1995.

INDEX

Children's B PARKS
Stoltman, Joan
Rosa Parks

07/24/18